YOU&GOD

THE ESSENTIAL PRAYER DIARY

ELAINE CARR

With thanks to the young people @ Deeper,
Letchworth Christian Fellowship's youth group, for
all their Us2 comments.

Copyright © Elaine Carr 2004
First published 2004
Reprinted 2005
ISBN 1 84427 025 4

Scripture Union, 207–209 Queensway, Bletchley, Milton Keynes, MK2 2EB, England.
Email: info@scriptureunion.org.uk
Website: www.scriptureunion.org.uk

Scripture Union Australia
Locked Bag 2, Central Coast Business Centre, NSW 2252
Website: www.su.org.au

Scripture Union USA
PO Box 987, Valley Forge, PA 19482
www.scriptureunion.org

Scriptures quoted from The Youth Bible, New Century Version (Anglicised Edition) copyright © 1993 by Nelson Word Ltd., 501 Nelson Place, P.O. Box 141000, Nashville, TN 37214-1000, USA.

British Library Cataloguing-in-Publication Data.
A catalogue record of this book is available from the British Library.

Printed and bound in Great Britain by CPI Bath Press, Bath.

Cover design: Hurlock Design

❧ Scripture Union is an international Christian charity working with churches in more than 130 countries, providing resources to bring the good news about Jesus Christ to children, young people and families and to encourage them to develop spiritually through the Bible and prayer.

As well as our network of volunteers, staff and associates who run holidays, church-based events and school Christian groups, we produce a wide range of publications and support those who use our resources through training programmes.

This is going to be *great*!

It's just you and God, talking about stuff which really matters to you. And get this: when you pray, the God of the whole universe stops to listen… not only does he *listen*, but he also answers and acts… How awesome is that?!

So are you ready to talk? And are you ready to listen?

Your name: Sarah Ritchie

Your address: 42 Woodlands Park

Rosemount, Blairgowrie

Scotland

Your age: 16

Date you start this diary: 22 - 7 - 06

How this works...

There are 70 prayer stops in your diary. Start with prayer stop 1 today. Then choose your route:

- you can do prayer stop 2 tomorrow, 3 the next day, 4 the next... and carry on going through the book. Leave the **Backtrack boxes** blank for the time being ~ they'll make sense when you backtrack @ prayer stop 7.
- you can choose the tracks you're most interested in, and follow those. BUT remember to backtrack after every six prayer stops.
- you can 'freestyle', choosing the prayer stops you want to make in any order you like. BUT you do need to backtrack after every six prayer stops!

You could shade in the prayer stops as you make them on this chart ~ that way, you'll be able to see how far you've come!

YOU	FRIENDS	FAMILY	SCHOOL	FUN	MONEY & STUFF	BELONGING	YOU MEETS WORLD	SECRET YOU	LOVE
1	2	3	4	5	6	BACK TRACK	8	9	10
11	12	13	BACK TRACK	15	16	17	18	19	20
BACK TRACK	22	23	24	25	26	27	BACK TRACK	29	30
31	32	33	34	BACK TRACK	36	37	38	39	40
41	BACK TRACK	43	44	45	46	47	48	BACK TRACK	50
51	52	53	54	55	BACK TRACK	57	58	59	60
61	62	BACK TRACK	64	65	66	67	68	69	BACK TRACK

help! I don't think I'll get round to this...

OK, so we've all got mega busy lives with loads of stuff going on… but praying is important… and *so* worth it! Each of these prayer stops will take you about ten minutes ~ that's about the same amount of time it'll take you to unwrap and eat a chocolate bar or watch a quarter of a TV programme! It'll work best for you if you pick a regular time to make your prayer stops ~ like as soon as you get in from school… or just before you go to bed. Choose a time which will work for you *now* and write it here ~

…and ask for God's help to stick to it!

PS If you miss a day or two, *don't* worry… just pick it up again and keep going…!

Us2 When I first started praying, it didn't feel right because I was thinking, 'OK, I'm talking to the air!' It doesn't make sense and you don't feel like anybody's listening. But over time, things start to happen and you realise, 'hey, somebody *is* listening!' You mustn't ever give up… *Hayley*

What's in it...

Secret you		**Love**	
9.	happy	10.	God is love
19.	stress-ometer	20.	the WOW! feelings
29.	scary!	30.	I fancy…
39.	understood	40.	going out
59.	you've got an attitude…	50.	uh oh…
69.	dreams	60.	hold on

You **backtrack** @ 7, 14, 21, 28, 35, 42, 49, 56, 63 and 70.

You can get help on these issues ~

I don't think I'll get round to this…	↗ the previous page…!
I don't know what words to use!	↗ 4
How do I hear God?	↗ 7
Why praise God?	↗ 10
My mind's all over the place!	↗ 16
God isn't answering!	↗ 21, 28
Why say sorry?	↗ 25
What do I do when God speaks?	↗ 42
I'm struggling to keep going…	↗ 56, 58
What do I pray if someone gets really ill?	↗ the space at the back

There are messages from other young people who are into prayer under the **Us2** logo ~

And there's *more* space for you at the back ~

Fill this space with stuff about you ~ what you like, what you don't like... what you do, what you want to do... *anything* which says *something* about *you* now. Use colour, cartoons, symbols, graffiti... maybe even paste in a photo ~ it's your space!

"LORD,
you have examined me and know all about me ~
you are all around me — in front and at the back
— and have put your hand on me ~
you made my whole being — you formed me in my
mother's body… you made me in an amazing and
wonderful way!"

David, talking to God [Psalm 139:1,5,13]

Or look at it this way ~

God knows you.
God is with you.
God is for you.
God created you.

Just stop and think: how **real** do those things seem to
you now?

pray something like this:

Thanks, Lord! Please help me to really get this
~ that you designed me, that you know and
understand me, that you love me ~ totally.

And before you go, try and memorise those four facts
~ but put 'me' instead of 'you'. Say them to yourself
today ~ often.

BACKTRACK BOX

God knows me
God is with me
God is for me
God created me

Next stop on this track: 11

who are your best mates?

List them here and say what you like about them... add a sketch, photo or cartoon, if you want ~

If you don't feel you've got any real friends right now, skip this ~ try 17 instead...

Naomi Ward.

She is my best friend & she is a good laugh to be around.

Nikita

Nikita is a great laugh & it is hard to be sad or upset around her!

Friends are great, aren't they? And actually, you don't just get good mates... God gives them to you. So stop ~ and thank him for each of your friends.

Now think about what's going on in their lives right now ~ what do you think they need from God? Try and say something for each of your friends here ~

Talk with God about each of these situations ~ ask him to get involved and change them.

"When a believing person prays, great things happen."

James, Jesus' brother, said that (and he should know!) [James 5:16] ~ your prayers **will** make a difference!

— **BACKTRACK BOX** ◄

Next stop on this track: 12

OK, so they might sometimes make Homer Simpson look caring, understanding and sorted, but let's face it, your parent(s) are very important in your life. So how's your relationship with them right now? Draw a line to link the person with the statement which best sums it up for you ~ or use the empty boxes to say it in your own words ~

	We get on great. They're like my best friend.
Mum	They just haven't got a clue about my life or what's important to me...
Dad	Total nightmare.
Step-mum	It's good. We argue sometimes, but generally it's OK.
Step-dad	I love them, but they stress me out big time.
	It used to be great. I don't know why, but we just don't seem to get on any more...

Cross out or add to fit your family!

US2

There's been a bit of conflict with my mum and dad recently, so I just started praying about it because I thought it'd be really bad if we were all just bickering with each other all the time. I said, 'I don't know what to do about this, God, so can you just bring my family back together a bit and help me to be more patient and stuff?' And he really did start to change it around ~ it wasn't just me making an effort. It's really brought us back to getting along. *Leah*

thanks!

However you feel right now, there's lots of good stuff about your parent(s)! Think it, write it and pray it now ~

Thanks, Lord...

help!

Ask for God's help with the things which you find tough ~

Please, Lord...

The bottom line is... God wants you to *respect* your parent(s) [See Exodus 20:12] ~ will you do that?

sorry!

Let's be honest ~ we all do things which hurt our parent(s). Sort them out now ~

Sorry, Lord...

— BACKTRACK BOX ◄

Next stop on this track: 13

How has school been for you over the last few days? Circle one!

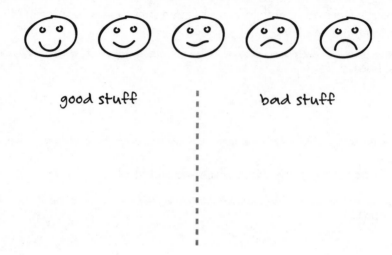

good stuff

bad stuff

Do you ever talk with God about this stuff? I mean, really talk it through with him? He is interested in *every* part of your life! Take some time to do that now. Tell him how you feel about things… Ask for his advice… Maybe imagine him sitting on that chair next to you ~ or go for a walk and imagine him there beside you…

help! I don't know what words to use…
Listen: there aren't any special words you need to learn. It's not like we have to try and impress God with a whole load of clever language! God totally understands plain-speak ~ and actually he also understands your thoughts and your feelings when you run out of words! Get this as well ~ the Holy Spirit is praying *with* us…! [Check this out in Romans 8:26–27]
  So relax. Just talk…

BACKTRACK BOX ◄

No school. No homework. No stuff to do around the house. Your time is your own… So what are you watching, reading, playing, listening to right now?

Top 3 CDs

1

2

3

Top 3 computer games

1

2

3

Top 3 books

1

2

3

Top 3 magazines

1

2

3

Top 3 TV programmes

1

2

3

Top 3 films

1

2

3

OK, so there's probably loads of good stuff there, but let's be honest ~ not everything we watch, read, play or listen to is that great… And actually, it really does matter ~ those things stay in our minds and hearts, and have the power to shape our thoughts and feelings. So here's how to pray out the rubbish:

1. Ask the Holy Spirit to show you anything that's not right.

2. Start by looking over your 'Top 3s' ~ does anything make you feel uncomfortable? Be honest about it by writing it here!

3. Tell God you're sorry about watching or reading or playing or listening to whatever it is…

4. Ask God to take away any wrong thoughts or feelings or worries.

5. Make a choice ~ how are things going to be different from now on?

6. Tell God about your decision… and ask for his help ~ you'll need it!

BACKTRACK BOX ◄

"Create in me a pure heart, God, and make my spirit right again."
David [Psalm 51:10]

> "God richly gives us everything to enjoy."
>
> Paul writing to Timothy
> [1 Timothy 6:17]

Wow. Read that a couple of times… what hits you about it?

So get up and look around your room ~ look in all the cupboards, on all the shelves, under the bed (OK, maybe not!)… You probably see this stuff loads of times a day, but now *really* look at it! Then go and have a look around the kitchen ~ check out what there is to eat in the fridge… while you're at it, check out *who* and *what* is in the living room…

look at **everything God has given you!**

Now, what do you want to say to him?

┌─ **BACKTRACK BOX** ◄──────────────────

Next stop on this track: 16 ▶

... he doesn't always do things in the way we expect! If you've been praying ~ which you have ~ then God has been listening... and he *will* answer. Sometimes it's a *'right now, right there in front of you'* kind of an answer. But often it's more like: *'wait... and look carefully'* ~ and it's so easy to miss those!

So take time to go back over what you've been praying ~ ask God to go with you, of course! Look again at the last six prayer stops you've made. Note down in the **Backtrack boxes** anything which God has changed or has shown you. Maybe you need to pray again about some things?

So... what's happening?

help! How do I hear God...?

... you need to listen! Obvious, but essential! Tell God you want to know what he has to say ~ and make space for him. Tune into:

• the Bible... read it often and think about what you read...

• wisdom from other people, like your youth leader...

• the Holy Spirit ~ fast-track to 58 for more about how he speaks...

And always, *always* check out what you think God is saying to you with someone you trust.

Guess what? God wants *you* to be an influencer. That's not arrogant or show off-y. And you don't have to be Mr/Ms Loud-with-loads-of-friends. It's for all of us. It's part of being a Christian.

But don't panic. You don't have to make it happen all by yourself. Jesus has sent his Holy Spirit ~ your bit is to work with his power, step out and be who you're designed to be!

So pray something like this ~ fill in the gaps as you go!

It's in Matthew 5:13–16, if you want to check it out!

Jesus, you said that you wanted me to be salt and light ~ to make a difference where I am. That makes me feel…

Please give me your Holy Spirit ~ fill me with your power, and make me a positive influence.

Lord, I know that I can be influenced by…

Please help me to see when that goes too far ~ help me to know how to draw the line and be myself.

— BACKTRACK BOX ◄

Next stop on this track: 18

How happy are you at the moment? Where would you put yourself along this line?

REALLY HAPPY ———————————————— **REALLY DOWN**

Maybe you feel like you whizz up and down that line ~ feeling good one minute, feeling horrible the next…

The fact is that God wants to hear from us, whatever mood we're in. David ~ who wrote lots of the songs in the Bible ~ had really got this sorted. So let's learn from him!

Choose now:

Feeling fab?   **Feeling down?**

Top tip: don't forget about God when life is good ~ enjoy it with him!

Start here:

> "I will praise you, Lord, with all my heart.
> I will tell of all the miracles you have done.
> I will be happy because of you;"
>
> David, talking to God [Psalm 9:1–2]

Say what you're happy about ~ try using lines like in a song, if you want:

Read it back to God again ~ maybe sing it, dance it, mime it too!

Top tip: don't feel bad about feeling bad! And don't try to sort things yourself and then talk to God about them! God wants you to share your feelings and problems with him.

Start here:

"Lord, listen to my words.
Understand my sadness.
Listen to my cry for help, my King and my God,
because I pray to you."

David, talking to God [Psalm 5:1–2]

Say what's making you unhappy ~ try using lines like in a song, if you want:

However you feel right now, God is still good... Can you say you still trust him?

"But let everyone who trusts you be happy."

David, talking to God [Psalm 5:11]

"Anyone who is having troubles should pray.
Anyone who is happy should sing praises."

[James 5:13]

BACKTRACK BOX

Next stop on this track: 19

... three small words = one MEGA fact!!! God's love is absolutely *huge* ~ we could spend our whole lives trying to get our heads round it... and there would still be *loads* more to experience and learn! So let's focus on God's love ~ it's the most important thing you'll do this week!

You can do this *or* this... or maybe this *and* this!

one

Maybe you know this song...? Circle the words which describe what God's love is like or what God's love does ~ do they say it for you too...?

Your love is amazing
Steady and unchanging
Your love is a mountain
Firm beneath my feet
Your love is a mystery
How you gently lift me
When I am surrounded
Your love carries me

Fill the space with your own ideas ~ and maybe add lines from songs *you* like about God's love...

Now turn the page...

two

Where has God shown *you* his love? Think about what you've seen in *Jesus*, in *your life* and in the *world* ~ fill the space with words or symbols, and lines to link your ideas…

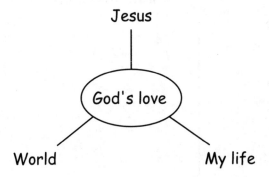

Jesus

God's love

World   My life

Now turn the page…

praise God!

Look back over what you've thought and written… use it to ~

Say to   **GOD**   what his   **LOVE**   is like to you.

Thank   for his   .

Ask   to help you experience his   more.

← **BACKTRACK BOX**

why praise…?

Praise… is getting caught up in the excitement of knowing God… it's telling God how much he means to you…

And actually praise does you good! It works like a boomerang ~ if I tell God he's love, I know that I'm loved… if I tell God he's powerful, I know that I'm safe… if I tell God he's faithful, I know I'm never going to be let down… get the idea?

Grab two different coloured pens, find a mirror ~ and have a good look at yourself! Take one colour and note around this body shape what you like about yourself ~ then take the other colour and say what you don't like…

PS If all you wrote was negative, go and talk about that with someone you trust…

Use this prayer to kick-start your conversation with God:

> Lord, you made my whole being; [Read Psalm 139:13] ~
> So please help me to like and look after myself ~ but not so much I get big-headed… [Read 1 Timothy 4:8]
> Lord, you are a God who heals ~
> So please keep me strong and healthy…
> Lord, you want to live in me [Read 1 Corinthians 3:16 or 6:19!] ~
> So please help me take care of myself ~ I don't want to do anything stupid with my body…

Next stop on this track: 31

What happens when you lose it with someone close to you? Are you a shout-and-scream sort of person? Or more of a sulk-quietly-in-your-room type?

Scribble down here what happened when you last fell out with someone important in your life. What was it about? How did you feel? What did you do? How did it all end up?

There are squillions of different ways to sort situations like that. But here's one thing you'll need, whatever:

FORGIVENESS

God asks us to *forgive* people who hurt us. That's tough. It's much easier to get your own back! But, like everything God asks us to do, it actually does us good. When you've really *forgiven* someone, you stop having negative thoughts and feelings about them ~ and let's face it, bad thoughts and feelings aren't a lot of fun! *Forgiveness* gives you freedom.

Forgiveness is a huge deal. Remember that Jesus included it in the prayer he taught us?

"Forgive us for our sins, just as we have forgiven those who sinned against us..."

[Jesus in Matthew 6:12]

Did you get that? Jesus is assuming that we've *forgiven* people...! So let's stop and check that we have.
(By the way, *forgiveness* doesn't mean letting someone carry on hurting you... If you're in a situation like that, get out of it ~ *fast*! And get help from someone you trust.)

Forgiveness can be a process. Are you ready to take some steps?

Go and get some stones, if you can. Think of anything that anybody has done to you which still hurts. Choose a stone for each thing you think of. Hold the stones – or you might have just one! ~ in your hand. Now go out somewhere. Take each stone in turn and tell God how you feel about the situation. Then tell him you want to forgive that person ~ and ask for his help. As a sign that it's happening, throw the stone as far as you can ~ be careful where, though!! ~ or bury it. Then walk away and leave it behind… how does that feel?!

Write the names of the people you think of on these stone shapes…

BACKTRACK BOX

US2

When I was younger, I was sexually abused. I became a Christian, but I was still holding on to unforgiveness. I'd buried it right deep down inside. One day I felt God tell me to forgive the man who'd abused me. That's changed my life. It was like I'd walked out of a prison. I know it's hard, I really do know it's hard, but even if you feel you can't forgive, God can help you to do it. By holding on to it, you are carrying pain with you wherever you go, but forgiveness releases you because you don't have to carry that pain. You're the one that's free. *Melissa*

Next stop on this track: 22

If you could ask God to change *three* things for your family right now, what would they be? Think people as individuals, think your family as a whole:

1.

2.

3.

So go ahead and ask him…

BACKTRACK BOX

... you're doing great!

Maybe you've already discovered that prayer is sometimes easy... but sometimes hard ~ and that hundreds of things will get in the way of you actually doing it! *But keep going!* With every prayer, you get closer to God. And as you touch heaven, God changes things here on earth...

So go back over the last six prayer stops you've made. Take your time... think carefully...
• Fill the **Backtrack boxes** with stuff God has said or done ~ and thank him for his answers!
• But you'll probably have some empty **Backtrack boxes**... Don't worry *at all* about that. Praying isn't like putting in an order at McDonalds! Keep talking with God about those things ~ God has heard you and he is doing something!

 I was doing really, *really* bad at history and when the exams came round, I started to panic. I was asking, 'God, can you help me out?' I sat the exam and I wrote loads. When the questions came up I just knew what to write... *Carla*

Your turn!
Here's your space to say how God has answered something you've prayed... txt it or e-mail it to a friend ~ or hey, just talk to them about it!

"**Give thanks** to the Lord because **he is good.**
His love continues for ever."

[Psalm 136:1]

Backtrack again after 6 more prayer stops @ 21

15) play!

Circle what's true for you!

Do you **play**...

... sport?	loads!	some...	what me ~ move?!
... computer stuff?	loads!	some...	are you kidding?
... cards, chess, board games...?	loads!	some...	board? Bored, more like!

Do you **play** to win? too right! don't mind... nah ~ it's just a laugh.

Maybe games are just a fun way for you to chill out. But if you're really into sport or something, you'll want to take it a bit more seriously...
So choose ~

If play only = fun

Remember that **all** the good stuff in our lives comes from God [~ check out James 1:17!]. So thank him for the times you've enjoyed playing whatever it is you play! Don't just make it a one-liner, though ~ God is interested in everything in your life...

Thanks, Lord...

Stop and **think** a bit more if:
· Your idea of being active is switching the TV remote...
· You're horrible when you win...
· You can't take it when you lose!
Maybe there's some stuff there to change with God's help. Ask him to get to work on you!

Please, Lord...

If play = serious stuff

Check out these three soundbites from Christians involved in sport:

• 'I regard my ability as a gift from God...' *Gavin Peacock, football*

If you're really good at something you play, then that's a talent *God has given you* ~ so *thank him* for it and *tell him* what it means to you ~

• 'When I run, I feel God's pleasure...' *Eric Liddell, athletics*

If you'd like to make God happy when you run, swim, score a goal or whatever it is you do ~ *tell him!*

• 'It's not so much how far I jump that glorifies God... it's more in the way I come across as I win or lose...' *Jonathan Edwards, triple-jump*

Talk with God about having the right attitude when you play ~

And think about this:

• 'The simple fact is that most sport for teenagers is on Sunday. You don't get a choice ~ if your team plays on Sunday, you either play on Sunday or you don't play at all.

So, pray about it and do what you think is right. If you do decide to play on Sunday, explain your decision to your church leaders. And look for another time in the week to get Christian teaching.' *Stuart Weir, Christians in Sport*

That's great advice!

Money is a *huge* deal with God ~ what we do with what we've got and how we are about what we *haven't* got! You might only get a bit of pocket money now, but this is a great time to get your attitudes sorted.

Prayer is a two-way thing, right? It's not like you need to do all the talking…! So this time, start by *listening*.

Stop.

Take your time.

Tell God you want to hear what he's got to say.

Now read. S-l-o-w-l-y.

And think…

"Don't store treasures for yourselves here on earth where moths and rust will destroy them and thieves can break in and steal them. But store your treasures in heaven where they cannot be destroyed by moths or rust and thieves cannot break in and steal them. **Your heart will be where your treasure is.**

No one can serve two masters. The person will hate one master and love the other, or will follow one master and refuse to follow the other. **You cannot serve both God and worldly riches.**

Don't worry and say, 'What will we eat?' or 'What will we drink?' or 'What will we wear?' The people who don't know God keep trying to get these things, and **your Father in heaven knows you need them. The thing you should want most is God's kingdom and doing what God wants.** Then all these other things you need will be given to you."

[**Jesus** talking to a crowd in Matthew 6:19–34]

Now it's your turn: what do you want to say to God about this? What do you want to change with his help?

Talk with God about it!

help! My mind's all over the place when I pray...
It is? So is mine!! Help yourself by getting rid of as many distractions as you can ~ like the TV, loud music, magazines, your mobile, other people... And don't lie down to pray ~ especially at the end of the day! But when you've done all this and you're talking with God, then suddenly realise you're wondering what's for dinner... stop yourself, say sorry to God, and carry on praying ~ I think God understands, don't you?!

Next stop on this track: 26

Picture a football match. On the sidelines is a guy who watches the same player all the time. It's not that the player is a total star. In fact, the others in the team don't always think the player is that great. But that doesn't matter: to look at the guy on the sidelines, you'd think the player was the best in the world!

Whenever the player gets the ball, the guy on the sidelines cheers like *mad!*

If the player gets hurt, the guy looks like he really cares… he's there straightaway to pick the player up and set him right.

And when the player messes up, the guy on the sidelines looks like he knows how it feels. People might laugh or criticise or shout insults... but he never does. All the guy wants to do is help the player get it sorted and get on with enjoying the game...!

Other people come and watch the player sometimes. But the guy on the sidelines is *always* there – whatever.

That's one of the best ways I've ever heard to describe how God is with us! Think about it a bit: the match represents everything you do in your life, the guy on the sidelines is God… the player is *you*.

Sometimes we think God behaves like other people in our lives. Like he's really hard to please. Or like he just puts up with us. Or maybe like he wants to make us feel bad when we mess things up.

But that's not how it is at all. God accepts us totally, just as we are. He's not saying, 'Get yourself sorted, then I'll get interested…' God cheers when we do well (and that's much more often than you'd think!). And when things aren't that great, he *really* feels for us and wants to help ~ even when we're at fault.

God accepts you totally. You belong with him.

OK, now be honest. Is that really how you feel God is with you? Write to him about this ~

Dear Father God,

Next stop on this track: 27

Stuck for ideas?

· Read the scene at the football match again, this time thinking about yourself as the player and God on the sidelines...

· Ask God to help you feel sure that he accepts you totally ~ tell him why you sometimes find it hard to believe that he does...

· Thank God that he accepts you completely, just as you are...

You can do it! Yep, you!! You don't have to be US President, a TV celebrity, an aid worker in a poor country ~ or even an adult! ~ to make a difference to people's lives.

Just think about *all* the people you see or talk with… put more names around the circle until it pretty much includes everyone in your life…!

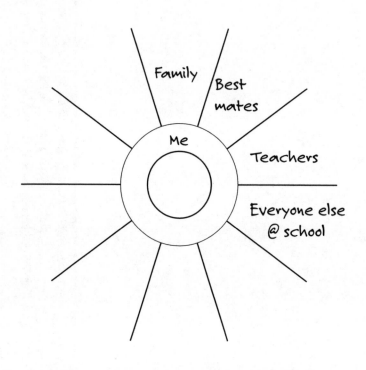

How many people is that altogether? Loads! The fact is, you *are* an influence on them ~ but whether it's a good influence or not is up for grabs…

OK, so how do we pray about this?

1. get power

There are loads of really good people around doing loads of really good stuff for their friends, community, nation ~ or even the world!! You might be able to think of some. But doing things in God's power ~ and not on your own ~ has got to be a fantastic advantage, right?!

Jesus said,

> "when the Holy Spirit comes to you, you will receive power"
>
> [Acts 1:8]

and

> "your heavenly Father [will] give the Holy Spirit to those who ask him"
>
> [Luke 11:13]

So go ahead. Ask God to give you *more* of his Holy Spirit ~ believe and receive!

And write 'The Holy Spirit' in the centre circle to remind you how important this is!

2. choose to act

Pray about the people in your circle. Think of positive things to say or do for them ~ be open to what God has to say…

Unless God says something *huge*, go for do-able things. Don't think 'world peace and an end to all bullying by next Tuesday…' Think things like:
• being there for a friend who's having a hard time…
• helping out a bit more at home ~ hey, you could even tidy your room!!! (PS If you do, try not to look like you're having your teeth pulled without an anaesthetic!)
• telling someone in a non-cheesy way about you and Jesus…
Add the things that come to your mind around the circle.

'Preach the Gospel at all times. If necessary, use words.'

[Francis of Assisi ~ he lived a long time ago, but man, he was smart!!]

In other words, *everything* you do in the *power* of the **Holy Spirit** will point people to **God**… how cool is that?!!

Put crosses in the boxes from 1 to 10 to show how stressed you feel at the moment about each of these things ~ 1 = totally laid back... 10 = seriously stressed! Then use the boxes to say *exactly* what the deal is.

school stuff  1 2 3 4 5 6 7 8 9 10

What's stressful?

family stuff  1 2 3 4 5 6 7 8 9 10

What's stressful?

friends stuff  1 2 3 4 5 6 7 8 9 10

What's stressful?

love stuff 1 2 3 4 5 6 7 8 9 10

What's stressful?

other stuff  1 2 3 4 5 6 7 8 9 10

What's stressful?

Now this might seem a weird thing to do next, but go with it!

Think about how great God is… let your mind get round how powerful, how trustworthy, how all-knowing, how loving he is...

It might help you to play a worship song or read a bit of the Bible or go out and look at the world…

The point is… if we fill our heads with what God is like, the things which stress us don't seem quite so big. God can handle them, don't you think?

That's not to say those things don't matter to God ~ they do.

> Give all your worries to him, because he cares about you.
> Peter writing to Christians in trouble... [1 Peter 5:7]

Talk with God about the things which are stressing you. And keeping talking with him as you hit those stressful situations today. He wants to help ~ and he can help.

US2 During my exams, I just prayed that God would kind of separate out the different exams for me, because I was having problems and I'd got so much information in my head. I prayed and said, 'I really need you to help me get it all straight.' He did that and I got good results. *Jamie*

— **BACKTRACK BOX** ◄

Next stop on this track: 29

The guy says: My darling, you are beautiful! Oh, you are beautiful...!

The girl says: I am weak with love. My lover's left hand is under my head, and his right arm holds me tight...

[From the Bible ~ yes, really! Song of Solomon 1:15; 2:5–6]

Wow! If you ever thought God wasn't into passionate, intimate, dizzy love between a man and a woman ~ think again!

Maybe you've already felt really special about someone else... but maybe you haven't. Maybe you'd love to fall in love... or maybe the whole idea seems *yucky!*

Falling in love is a *fantastic* experience God has for most of us at some time in our lives! It may be a way off, but God is already working on you ~ if you'll cooperate with him *now*, he'll make you the kind of person who can *really* love someone else. So, get into training ~ practise being loving. And pray like this:

> Father God ~
> Those amazing feelings of falling in love
>   are a gift from you ~ thank you!
> While I'm waiting,
>   please make me more loving.
> Help me think about others ~
>   and not always myself!
> Make me
>   more giving,
>   much kinder,
>   and more forgiving.
> Make me
>   less selfish,
>   and not so thoughtless.
> I'll try hard, but there's no way I'll do it without you!
> You are love.
>   Show me how to be more like you.

Next stop on this track: 30

fantastic!!

You know how this bit works by now! Go back over the last six prayer stops you've made and fill in the **Backtrack boxes** with stuff that God has done or said…If you've got time, go back further and see what's happened in the situations you prayed about at the start...

Is everything sorted then? I'd be surprised!

help! God isn't answering…! (Part 1)

Some prayer-answers are just round the corner. Others are much further away ~ I'll guarantee there are some of those in your life!

Jesus told a story about a woman who *kept on asking* a judge to sort something for her ~ and finally she got what she wanted. He said it's like that with

> It's in Luke 18:1–8 if you want to check it out…!

God and prayer sometimes. Not because we need to nag God ~ or work on him until we get our own way ~ or fight for his attention. Some things just take a long time. And in the process God is building our *trust* in him ~ and that's *really* important.

What do you need to *keep praying* about?

It works! (slowly, sometimes…)

I've been praying for my dad to get to know God for years ~ and I mean years…! He doesn't ~ yet. But things have happened. Like I can talk about God ~ and Dad listens… and looks kind of interested…! And he's come to things @ church a couple of times. God is answering my prayers ~ a bit at a time.

So what have I got to do now? **KEEP PRAYING**!!!

There is another reason why God might not *seem* to be answering…. We'll look at that when we backtrack next time.

Meanwhile, *keep praying*!

Backtrack again after 6 more prayer stops @ 28

So which of your friends don't yet know God? You might have loads! But just list three or four of your closest not-yet-Christian mates here:

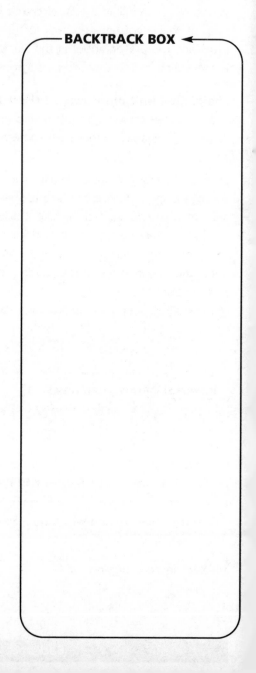

BACKTRACK BOX

The truth is, God really wants those people to get to know him ~ it's dead important that they do…! God is definitely doing stuff in their lives to get them to think about him. And you can be a *big* part of that:

- by being open about you and Jesus…
- by looking out for events for not-yet-Christians ~ and inviting them to go with you…
- and by praying.

So pray for each of them now…

'More things are wrought by prayer than this world dreams of.'
A poet called Tennyson.

Or, in other words, prayer is so much more powerful than you might think! So go for it!

Father God,

You'll probably have to pray that prayer a lot before you see the answers ~ are you up for that?

To help you, get a photo or something to remind you of each of the friends on your list ~ or just write their names out large on separate bits of paper. Put the photos (or whatever!) somewhere you'll see them a lot ~ maybe tack them on the walls of your room or your cupboard or your mirror or your PC screen! Every time you notice them, pray that your friends get to know God.

US2

I prayed for an opportunity to invite friends to church. Three of them came and that was really cool! But they didn't just come, they came and stayed and stuck with it. I prayed for it to be brought up in conversation ~we were just talking about weekends and what we were doing at the weekend and stuff, and I just said that I was going to church on Sunday…
Amanda

I've been praying for encouragement from God and to know the right moment to talk to people about God. And I've been able to have the right words to say. Two of my friends have started coming to church, and there's another one who wants to come, too! *Sam*

Next stop on this track: 32

Remember the Jesus prayer? When people asked Jesus how to pray, what did he tell them to say right at the start? **[Check out Matthew 6:9 if you're not sure…!]**

Two little words. *Loads* of *mega* meaning.

What does God want you to know about him?
Don't answer yet! **Meditate…**

How does he want your relationship with him to be?
Don't answer yet! **Meditate…**

> ### *Meditating*
>
> · it's a special kind of prayer ~
>
> · it's when you think about something with God… really think about something… and then think about it some more!
>
> · it's the prayer equivalent of chewing gum (well, sort of!) ~ it takes some time BUT the more you chew, the more you get out of it!

So go away and think about what Jesus said…

Come back *much* later and draw or write what God shows you…

What do you want to say to him about this?

IMPORTANT PS!!

If our dads hurt us in any way, it's easy to get that experience confused with what God is like… **But God is totally the ideal dad.** Maybe that's what you need to pray about here ~ that your dad in heaven would help you get over anything your dad on earth has messed up…

BACKTRACK BOX ◄

Next stop on this track: 33

It's that time of year again. You've got that brown envelope in your hand... and your school report is inside. So how do you feel? Tick the box which says it best for you and follow the arrows to pray.

☐ Depressed ~ I seem to be better at things which aren't taught in school!

It's true, lots of people are excellent at stuff you don't do exams in! God gives everybody talents, so what are you good at?

☐ Nervous ~ I haven't done my best at school this year...

OK, be honest. What has stopped you doing well?

☐ Mixed ~ there'll be some good stuff, some not quite so good...

☐ Happy and confident ~ I do well at school.

God has given you talents. So what have you done well in?

Everything you **do** or **say** should be done to **obey Jesus your Lord**.

[Paul writing to some Christians in Colossae ~ Colossians 3:17]

Maybe fast-track to 34 after this!

Thank God for those things! Take your time. Think about each one in turn... think about how it feels to do well...

Next step ~ only do this if you really mean it! If you include God in what you're good at, he'll totally transform it. Tell God you want to use your talents *with* him and *for* him.

But remember: *who you are* is *loads* more important than *what you do*!

What needs to change? Talk with God about it ~ ask for his help to turn things around.

BACKTRACK BOX ←

Next stop on this track: 34

When did you have most fun at a party? Think birthdays, Christmas, weddings, sleepovers…

God is seriously into parties ~ people getting together and enjoying life is his idea in the first place!

But wise up. As you go to more parties with your mates, you'll start to hit some issues. Make your mind up *now* about where you'll draw the line on these things ~ if you don't, you're loads more likely to go along with the crowd when you're there!

Ask God to guide you now. For each of these issues, say what would be OK ~ and what wouldn't…

	Great!!!	**I don't think so…**

Drinking
what about alcohol, for example?

Smoking
would it be OK to try?

Drugs
what will you do if someone
offers you some?

Body contact
how close is close enough?

TV and films
like are 15-rated movies OK?

Anything else?
what you talk about ~ and
what you do …

If you've overstepped this line…
Own up to God about it now ~
Know that, in Jesus, you have total forgiveness and a fresh start! [See 1 John 1:9]

why say sorry?

The things we do wrong mess up our friendship with God. If we want to be close with him, we need to own up ~ *and* choose *not* to keep making the same mistakes!

So… when is your next party?

Ever thought about praying before you go? Ask God to help you have a fantastic time. Also, ask him to help you walk away from anything which isn't that great… that way, you'll really party!

To make this a habit, write **P** (for pray!) by any kind of party in your diary… *or* on a post-it and stick it to what you'll wear!

ENJOY!!!

I'd been going out with this guy for two weeks and I'd broken up with him the day before we went to this festival. I just thought, 'God's going to tell me off because I've messed up *again*.' Then someone on stage said you don't need to sort yourself out to come to God ~ you *can't* sort yourself out ~ you need to let God sort you out. A lot of people think of God like a third parent ~ you go, say what you've done and get told off. But it's not like that. With God, you go, say what you've done and it gets sorted.   *Leah*

BACKTRACK BOX

Are you into shopping? Not 'filling a trolley with baked beans and loo roll'-type shopping. More 'wandering round and looking for stuff for *you*'-type shopping! So say a bit more ~

my favourite shops are...

I've recently got...

next, I'd love to get...

It's *great* to get things... and *great* to let God shape how we are about wanting stuff ~
So pray something like this:

> Lord, thanks for the money I get. Thank you for the things I've bought ~ and for the things people have bought me! Just help me keep it all in check...

'Whoever said money can't buy you happiness simply didn't know where to go shopping.'
[a famous-ish actress...!]

Sound... or sad?

BACKTRACK BOX

Next stop on this track: 36

Here's a chance to pray for your youth group. Write the name of the group inside the circle. Then write the names of the people in it ~ including the leaders ~ around the outside:

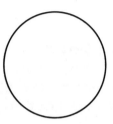

Now pray round that circle *twice* ~ pray for each person by name:

- for protection ~ like Jesus did: "keep them safe from the Evil One." [John 17:15]

- for God to show them what's best for them ~ like Paul did: "...asking God that you will know fully what he wants (...) so that you will live the kind of life that honours and pleases the Lord in every way." [Colossians 1:9–10]

When you're praying for someone, a word or a phrase or an image might come strongly to your mind ~ make a note of it by the person's name. And fast-track to 42 for some advice on what to do next!

BACKTRACK BOX

... is more than some people manage in a whole lifetime!!

Backtrack over the last six prayer stops you've made and note down in the boxes what God has said or done... Stop to:
- thank him for his answers;
- pray again about things which aren't sorted yet...

help! God isn't answering...! (Part 2)

The easiest way to get this idea is to hang around a 2-year old for a bit...! They might be dead cute, but the things they ask for ~ like no bedtime or non-stop biscuits! ~ aren't always best for them, are they?!

It's like that with the stuff we pray for sometimes ~ it might seem great to us, but it might not be the right thing from God's point of view... And God's timing is different from ours.

There's a line in the prayer Jesus taught:

In other words, 'God, *you* know best.
I trust you to do what's right even if
it means I don't get what I asked for...'

That's a tough prayer to pray ~ and really mean. It takes faith ~ and courage.

Think of all the things you're asking God for at the moment ~ can you pray 'your will be done' in them? Use this space to say what you think, feel or do next ~

PS Remember, there are other reasons why you might not have your answer to prayer just yet... Backtrack to prayer stops 7 and 21 for a quick reminder!

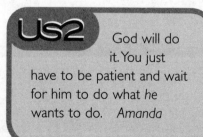
US2 God will do it. You just have to be patient and wait for him to do what *he* wants to do. *Amanda*

Anything with eight legs does it for me. And I'm not that great on aeroplanes either…

It's bad enough being arachnophobic (scared of spiders) and aerophobic (frightened of flying), but imagine what life would be like for an optiophobe ~ a person terrified of opening their eyes? Or a geniophobe ~ someone petrified of chins?!

How about you? What are you scared of? Take some time to list the things which make you feel frightened…

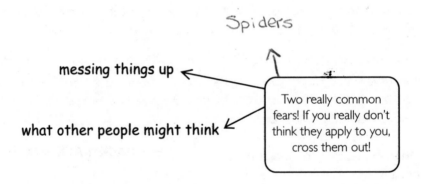

Spiders

messing things up

what other people might think

Two really common fears! If you really don't think they apply to you, cross them out!

Think about it… **Fear** is one of the most powerful emotions ~ it can:
• make you unhappy;
• stop you doing things which you'd really like to do… or which would be good for you;
• affect how you act (~ if you've ever seen an arachnophobe like me around a spider, you'll know fear makes you *weird*!!)

Not great, eh? So, not surprisingly, God has a lot to say about **fear**…

God said,

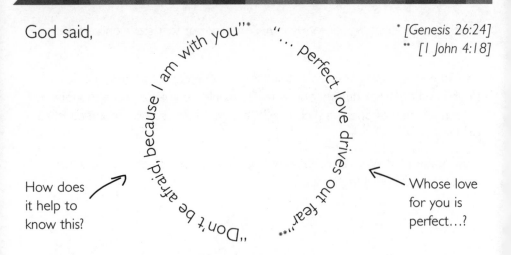

* [Genesis 26:24]
** [1 John 4:18]

"...perfect love drives out fear."**

"Don't be afraid, because I am with you"*

How does it help to know this?

Whose love for you is perfect...?

Read round the circle and think about the questions...

Look at your list of scary stuff over the page. Write each of your fears in the circle ~ talk with God about them as you go.

Now read round the circle again and hear God saying those things to *you*...

(If you're doing this at night, maybe go and get a torch... Switch out the lights and shine the torch over the circle as you write in your fears ~ it's just to remind you that prayer takes fear *out* of the darkness and *into* God's light!)

If **fear** is a big deal for you at the moment, try:

• writing DBABIAWY or PLDOF (the first letters of the words in the Bible text!) on a band and wear it round your wrist... or write them anywhere you'll see them loads (~ on your mirror, across the pages of your school planner...)

• checking out more Bible stuff on fear ~ Psalm 56:3 and 27:1 are great to start with...

• talking about your fears with someone you trust...

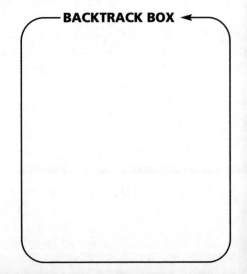

BACKTRACK BOX

who do you like at the moment? [maybe someone you know well, maybe someone you know at a distance, maybe someone famous…]

what do you like about him or her?

quick backtrack to prayer stop 20: all this exciting, dizzy love-stuff is God's idea… so let him in on it! Talk with God now about:

• who you like…

• your feelings… and what you do with them!

┌── **BACKTRACK BOX** ◄───────────────────────────┐
│   │
│   │
│   │
│   │
│   │
│   │
│   │
└──┘

Next stop on this track: 40 ▶

What are you like as a person? Loud or quiet? Fun or serious? Fill this space with words or pictures which describe your personality ~ be as creative as you like!

BACKTRACK BOX

Do you want to know what God is doing with your personality right now?

one: he's loving it!
This is 100 per cent true: God totally loves you as the person you are right now. He loves that mix of characteristics which is totally unique to you. Fantastic, eh?

Here's space to write a prayer to thank God for who you are. But maybe you don't feel so great about yourself... be honest with God about that ~ and ask him to help you see yourself the way he sees you!

Father God,

two: he's changing it...
If you're a Christian, God is @ work on you through the Holy Spirit. This is a you-and-God thing ~ he'll do the changing, but you've got to be willing to be changed!

Pray for *more* of the 'fruit' Paul writes about here... if any of the characteristics seem especially important, circle them as you go ~

But the Spirit produces the fruit of...

love   joy   peace   patience   kindness

goodness   faithfulness   gentleness   self-control...

[Paul writing to some Christians in Galatia ~ Galatians 5:22]

Look out for chances to *be* these things today!

Next stop on this track: 41

Got a stopwatch? Set it for 60 seconds… now *brainstorm*! Fill this space with your ideas about what a **friend** *is* or *does*… go!

Big idea: one of the things Jesus *can* be to us is a friend. A *really* good friend. Have you ever thought about him this way before? You may have heard it 100 times before, but have you *understood* what it means for your life?

Have another look at your brainstorm ~ what could be more a part of your relationship with Jesus? Take some time to *really* think about this in God's company… then circle two or three of the things you've written down.

And here's space to say something about that to Jesus ~ the best friend you could ever have…

Jesus,

PS – Do you know this prayer-song?

What a friend I've found
Closer than a brother
I have felt your touch
More intimate than lovers

Jesus, friend forever

What a hope I've found
More faithful than a mother
It would break my heart
To ever lose each other

Jesus, friend forever

Written by Martin Smith, © Curious? Music.
Rights administered by Bucks Music Ltd.
Lyrics reproduced by permission.

Sing it, play it or just say it ~ as a prayer.

BACKTRACK BOX

Next stop on this track: 52

What's true for you? [If your answer's different for your mum, dad, step-mum, step-dad, foster parents ~ or whoever looks after you ~ use a different colour code or symbol for each person.]

1. When it comes to what I *can* and *can't* do, my parents and I:

> • fight over most things;
>
> • talk about most things;
>
> • agree about most things.

2. If my parents make a rule I don't agree with, I'm most likely to:

> • break it;
>
> • try and talk it over with them;
>
> • go along with it ~ but make sure they know I'm *seriously* fed up!
>
> • go along with it ~ they probably know best anyway.

3. I think the rules my parents have for me are:

> • stupid and unreasonable;
>
> • *so* unfair ~ my friends can do loads more stuff than me!
>
> • mostly ~ but not always! ~ OK;
>
> • thoughtful and loving;
>
> • rules? What rules?!

You're getting your own ideas about what you want to do ~ and what you wouldn't want to do in a squillion years! That's totally normal. And actually, that's totally right for you as you move towards being an adult... But there can be a few fireworks with your mum and dad along the way, right?!

Get this: your parents *won't* always get it right. And that's especially true in this you're-not-a-kid-but-you're-not-quite-an-adult time. But we need to *respect* them, remember? [See Exodus 20:12] That means having an attitude which says, 'I'm *willing* to do what you ask… and I won't be a total brat about the things we disagree on!'

So think a bit more…

What do you and your parents fall out about most?

Are there rules you'd like to change? Why? How could that happen?

Are there attitudes and actions you need to say sorry for?

Now turn this into prayer ~ talk honestly with God about all this stuff. Be open to what he might have to say to you.

> **PS** Jesus was a teenager ~ and he had parents!!

BACKTRACK BOX

Next stop on this track: 43

Sports Day. I was down to represent my class at shot-put ~ which was weird, given I had the muscles of a gnat! But anyway, I stepped into the circle and picked up the shot (man, did it feel heavy!). *Everybody* was watching (well, that's how it seemed). But then the shot-thing fell out of my hand and hit the concrete circle with a massive thud, narrowly missing my toes. 'No throw!' shouted the teacher, loud enough for the *whole school* to hear (at least, that's how it felt). So off I walked whilst she wrote a huge, fat zero by my name. I wanted to crawl away and hide and never go back to school again…

Ever felt like that? Scribble down what happened when you messed up recently ~ go on, we've all done it!

Maybe you can just shrug your shoulders and laugh at that kind of experience ~ that's great! But our minds record those memories… sometimes with a message which says, 'You're no good…' or 'Don't try that again ~ you'll mess it up.'

Here's your chance to interrupt that message with the *truth*…

We all fail ~ sometimes. But you are not a failure! No way!! In fact, this is what God says to you:

> God has made us what we are.
> In Christ Jesus, God made us to do good works,
> which God planned in advance for us to live our lives doing.
>
> [from Ephesians 2:10]

Write your name in the box at the top. Then read that again. And again. And again – until you've memorised it. Now close your eyes and let those words replay in your mind. Let God say those things to *you*.

Here's your space to say what you share with God next ~

BACKTRACK BOX ◄

Backtrack over the past six days and think again about what God is doing or saying about the things you've prayed ~ write or draw some stuff in the boxes as you go…

Then backtrack some more! What has God changed?

Fantastic, isn't it?! This prayer stuff really works!

Stop and thank God for all that he's done so far!

> Come, let's sing for joy to the Lord.
> Let's shout praises to the Rock who saves us.
> Let's come to him with thanksgiving.
> Let's sing songs to him…
>
> [Psalm 95:1]

hey, there's an idea! Or let's dance for him, or write a poem for him, or draw for him, or play music for him…

US2

I can see now that prayers I prayed in the summer have been answered, but sometimes you don't know until you make the effort to look back… *Leah*

Backtrack again after 6 more prayer stops @ 42

Most people are trying hard to hang on to their money… but God asks us to give ours away! (Well, some of it, anyway.) Check out Deuteronomy 15:7,8 and 10–11, and 1 Corinthians 16:1–2.

Lots of Christians put aside 10% of the money they get and give it to the church. That's a great example to follow ~ so work out what 10% of your pocket money would be =

per week/month.

Could you hand that over to your church?

And what about people with less than you've got, materially? Think around the things you care about… and think creatively ~ like how about getting some friends together to sponsor a child in a poorer country?

You'll need to plan for this… otherwise it won't happen! So write a quick action plan. Then tell God what you're hoping to do ~ and why ~ and ask him to bless it.

Action plan:

...not yours! The Bible says the church is *like a body* ~ lots of different parts being happily active together... Is that how it is in *your* church?

Romans 12:4–5 and I Corinthians 12:14–20, if you want to check it out!

step one: reality check
The truth is, church can be great... but it can also be a **big** challenge! So ~

1. Circle which of these is truest for you.
2. Say a bit more in the box...
3. Then talk with God about it.

"Church is fantastic! I love it!"

"There's good stuff ~ and not-so-good stuff..."

"If I didn't have to go, I wouldn't."

"I'm not sure I fit in..."

"What's the point...?"

If you're *not* in a church at the moment, think hard about finding one. And if you *really* can't get on where you are, think about looking for somewhere else ~ *fast*! Church is good for you ~ *you* grow as you get from ~ and give to ~ other Christians.

US2
I came to church with Amanda and it was nice, but I saw everybody with their family. Without your family, you do feel kind of alone. The first time I prayed was that night. I prayed, 'Please God, I don't want to be alone...' The next Sunday I just felt so much at home. Loads of people started talking to me and I realised I didn't need my family there to feel at home... *Hayley*

... in Christ, **we are all one body**. Each one is a part of that body, and **each part belongs to all the other parts**...
[Paul, writing to some Christians in Rome ~ Romans 12:5]

step two: prayer

Prayer is one way to make a HUGE difference to what goes on in your church!
Try these actions, praying as you go ~

Head ~ put your hand on your head ~ pray for the **leaders** by name…

Mouth ~ put your hand on your mouth ~ pray for the **speakers** by name…

Heart ~ put your hand on your heart ~ pray for the **carers** by name (=
anybody who's there for people when the going gets tough…)

Hands ~ hold out your hands ~ pray for the **do-ers** by name (= anybody
who makes things happen!) Like who plans and runs the things you're involved
in? Who cleans the place?

Feet ~ touch your feet ~ pray for the **ambassadors** by name = people who
go out into your community or overseas to share God…

Hands again! ~ clasp your hands together ~ pray *for* **togetherness** and **one-
ness**… pray *against* arguments and splits in your church. (That's a really
important prayer! Jesus prayed it *just* before he was arrested. [See John 17:21])

BACKTRACK BOX ◄

…We're not talking Christmas or birthday prezzies here… we're talking spiritual gifts ~ the talents and abilities the Holy Spirit gives to Christians. What you unwrap on your big day will be great… but these are something else! So have a read of this letter, think about the stuff in the boxes… and *pray*!!!

Spot the gifts! As you read this, circle the different gifts and abilities ~ there are 16 of them here… Which has God given you…?

Research! Christians have different opinions about what some of these gifts mean for us today. Make a few phone calls, send a few e-mails, text or talk to somebody to find out what the guys @ your church think…

Dear Christians
   I want you to understand about spiritual gifts… There are different kinds of gifts, but they're all from the same Spirit. *There are different ways to serve, but the same Lord to serve.* And there are different ways that God works through people, but the same God. *Something from the Spirit can be seen in each person, for the common good.* The Spirit gives one person the ability to speak with wisdom, and the same Spirit gives another the ability to speak with knowledge. The same Spirit gives faith to one person. And, to another, that one Spirit gives gifts of healing. The Spirit gives to another person the power to do miracles, to another the ability to prophesy. And he gives to another the ability to know the difference between good and evil spirits. The spirit gives one person the ability to speak in different kinds of languages and to another the ability to interpret those languages. *One Spirit, the same Spirit, does all these things, and the Spirit decides what to give each person…*
   The person who has the gift of prophecy should use that gift in agreement with the faith. Anyone who has the gift of serving should serve. Anyone who has the gift of teaching should teach. Whoever has the gift of

What are spiritual gifts for?

Who gets spiritual gifts?

Prophecy ~ hearing from God about something and passing it on…

Where do you get spiritual gifts?

encouraging others should encourage. Whoever has the gift of giving to others should give freely. Anyone who has the gift of being a leader should try hard when he leads. Whoever has the gift of showing mercy to others should do so with joy.

> Yours
> Paul

What should you do with the gifts you are given?

[1 Corinthians 12:1,4–11 and Romans 12:6–8]

Did you get all that?! God gives gifts to *everyone* through his **Holy Spirit**. They are for you... but they're also for God and for other people. You can't buy them. You can't earn them. They're **not** badges for Super-Christians... They're totally a gift.

So here's what *we* do about spiritual gifts:
- Ask for them.
- Receive them.
- Use them to the max.

So **pray...**
- Take a minute to let your mind quieten down from all the stuff whizzing around it!
- Hold out your hands and *ask* God for a gift... take your time and remember, it's *his* choice!
- Tell him that you want to use your gifts *really* well.

BACKTRACK BOX ◄─────────────────────────────

Next stop on this track: 48

> ## Nobody understands me!!!

Have you ever said ~ or thought ~ something like that?

The truth is, it's *very* difficult for another person to know *exactly* how we feel about things… or to *really* get a hold of what's important to us.

But there is someone who can.

God.

Listen in for a moment on a conversation David had with God a l-o-n-g time ago…

> Lord,
> You know my thoughts
>   before I think them.
> You know thoroughly
>   everything I do.
> Lord,
> Even before I say a word,
> You already know it.

[Psalm 139:2–4]

Wow. Just think about that for a moment…

Not only does God understand what you *do*, but he also understands how you *think* and *feel*…

Not only does God understand what we *have* done, but he also understands what we *will* do…

How do you feel about that?

Turn your thoughts and feelings into a prayer, like David did ~

Lord,

BACKTRACK BOX

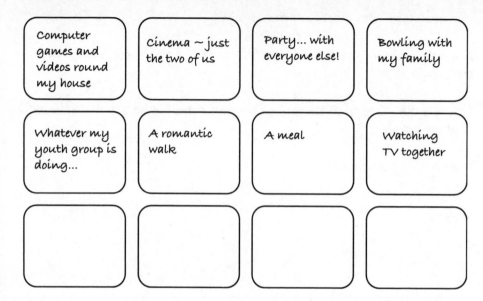

Computer games and videos round my house

Cinema ~ just the two of us

Party... with everyone else!

Bowling with my family

Whatever my youth group is doing...

A romantic walk

A meal

Watching TV together

Ideas for where to go and what to do with a girl or boyfriend ~ what do you think?
- Put a line through any you think are a total no-no!
- Circle the one you're most likely to go for...
- ...and add your own ideas in the empty boxes.

Going out with someone can be really cool! You'll need a sense of humour... stuff to say... things you both like... courage! Oh, and *wisdom*.

wisdom = what God thinks about something + what to do about it.

God loves to give us *wisdom* for this kind of stuff in our lives ~ check that out in James 1:5 if you've got a minute! So go ahead. Ask him to make you wise about who you go out with and what you do together.

PS God wants us to have the *best* time, the *best* friends, the *best* experiences! If you've never let God in on this bit of your life, do that now!

BACKTRACK BOX ◄

Sketch yourself here in your favourite clothes. Or draw yourself as you'd really like to look. Or cut out and stick in clothes, hair and stuff you like from magazines.

your image is not nothing...

Some people seem to think it's wrong to care about looking good... Well, God didn't make us like amoeba – shapeless blobs of jelly! Our bodies are God's creation ~ so we should enjoy *and* care for them!

your image is not everything...

Some people get really hung up about their appearance. It's as if looking cool is the most important thing in life. That's sad. It's who you are in God that really counts.

Take some time to answer these questions:

- How important is your image to you?

- How do you feel about your image right now?

- Whose ideas of what looks good influence you? Your gran's?! Your parents? Your friends? The in-crowd @ school? Magazines?

Feel confident with
         Enjoy ———————➤ **your image**… but don't let it be a big deal!
Have fun with

That's a great attitude to have ~ how close to it are you?

Now talk with God about each of your answers. Be honest about your thoughts and feelings ~ God really is interested. Oh, and remember to listen as well!

BACKTRACK BOX ◄

OK, here we go again! Backtrack over your last six prayer stops and think ~ what is God doing?
What has God been saying?
Fill in the boxes…
… then thank God for what he's done and pray some more into those not-yet-sorted situations.

help! What do I do when God speaks…?

When you're praying, an image might come strongly to your mind. Or an idea. Or a word. Or a line from a Bible text or a song… These are *some* of the ways God speaks to us.

If this hasn't happened for you yet, just keep listening! But if it has, make a note here of the prayer stop(s) where you got the strong image… or idea… or word… or Bible text…

Wow! God speaking to *you*. How cool is that??!!

This is the 'wisdom', 'knowledge' and 'prophecy' we read about @ prayer stop 38…! God gives it to us ~ and we're supposed to do something with it. So here we go!

step one: draw or write down carefully what God seems to be saying (~ don't get carried away and add bits!);

step two: pray about it:
• God might show you more…
• God might help you see what it means…
• God might tell you clearly what to do next…

step three: get in touch with someone you trust who's smart *and* experienced with this kind of stuff! Talk it through with them. Decide together what to do with what God has said:
• Do you need to pray about something in a new way?
• Do you need to act or think differently about something?
• Do you need to pass the message on to someone else?

PS
If what you've heard disagrees with what's in the Bible, forget it ~ it isn't from God.

Backtrack again after 6 more prayer stops @ 49

> The Lord says, "Whoever loves me, I will save.
> I will protect those who know me.
> They will call to me, and I will answer them.
> I will be with them in trouble;
> I will rescue them and honour them."
>
> [Psalm 91:14–15]

Isn't that a fantastic promise? Read it again, s-l-o-w-l-y... Hear God **promise** each of the *five* things to *you*.

Now...

Write the names of the people in your family in the middle of the next page. Or draw them. Or stick in a photo...

Round the edges, write or draw symbols for anything you feel threatens to upset things for your family right now.

Now pray ~ and I mean really pray! ~ for God's protection. As you do, write these words *round* your family...

> **You are my place of safety and protection. You are my God and I trust you.**
>
> [Psalm 91:2]

...write those words so that they surround your family and completely separate the people from the dangers... because that's what God's protection does for us ~ totally.

Go back and read the promise at the top again ~ that'd be a great Bible text to learn by heart, don't you think?

BACKTRACK BOX

Next stop on this track: 53

Just imagine it ~ *you* in the big comfy chair in the big, scary office! If you could run your school for a day, what would you change? Write down here any new rules you'd make… and any rules you'd get rid of for good!

Nice dream… Now back to reality!

How you handle authority is *really* important to God. Getting into trouble for busting the rules or giving teachers grief doesn't look great, does it? Remember: Jesus asks us to be like salt and light [Matthew 5:13–16]. That doesn't mean:

· just accepting *whatever* is going on ~ there *are* ways of getting things changed, right? (Try your year tutor or, if you have one, the school council, for example);

· losing all your cred with your friends ~ you can be a positive influence around school without being a total geek!

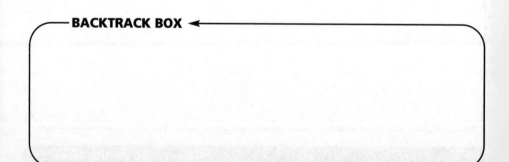

BACKTRACK BOX

So let's get this sorted...

rule-busting
Own up to God here about things you *do* which you *shouldn't*... and things you *don't do* which you *should*...

```



```

Be sorry.

Tell God what *you* are going to do to change...

```



```

And ask for his help.

teachers are human, too...
Yes, really! And even if you *never* get a detention, having a bad attitude towards someone is a big deal with God [Matthew 5:22]. So own up to God here about any of your teachers you have a problem with...

```



```

Be sorry.

Tell God what *you* are going to do to change...

```



```

And ask for his help.

Next stop on this track: 54

Think of *one* thing God has made ~ maybe an animal… or a place… or something you can see from your window right now… Draw or stick in a picture of whatever you're thinking of here:

• Is it made with imagination?

• Is it made with skill?

• Is it unique?

• Is it lovely?

God is *so* creative! And get this: whenever
you use
your imagination and skill
to
make something
or
express an idea
in pictures or words or music ~
you are joining in with what God does.

So here are some ways to be creative. Circle any that you do ~ even if only sometimes… and add any others you think of ~

Drama **Dance** **Design**

Writing **Music**
poems, stories, songs…

Making
anything! crafts, food, clothes,
models…

Art

Now finish these sentences ~ and use them to kick-start your conversation with God:

> Father God, thank you for all that you've made ~ I really like...
>
> Thanks for making me creative, too ~ I really enjoy...

if you're really into music or art or drama or design...
Imagine God giving you a huge box. Picture yourself opening it... inside are the things you need to be creative ~ like your musical instrument, paints, costumes... whatever fits with what you're good at!

The truth is that God gives us more than just the **tools**...! He gives us the **talent** and the **time** to use them... Stop and say something to God about this now.

And what do you *do* next? If you turn away and walk off with your gift ~ *stop!* God really wants you to enjoy it *with* him. Picture yourself doing that. Then think: how can you make that picture a reality...?
• how about talking with God when you're singing, playing, acting, drawing...?
• how about asking him to show you how to use your gift?
• anything else...?

BACKTRACK BOX

Your friends and family? Absolutely. Being happy? Yes. Doing well @ school or sport or music or…? That too. What else feels really important to you right now?

Here's a prayer-song. The writer has probably got *loads* going on in her life, too ~ but what's *most important* to her?

> Jesus, my passion in life is to know you,
> May all other goals bow down
>> to this journey of loving you more.
>
> Jesus, you've showered your goodness on me,
> You've given your gifts so freely,
>> but there's one thing I'm longing for ~
>
> Hear my heart's cry
>> and my prayer for this life ~
>
> Above all else
> Above all else
> Above all else
> Give me yourself.

Quick backtrack to 16 ~ can you link this with the last bit of what Jesus says? And can you spot the promise that goes with it…?

How do you feel about that?

This is *not* God saying your other stuff isn't important ~ no way!

But there *is* something *very* powerful in a prayer which says, 'These things are really important to me, Lord ~ but I want *you* first.'

Could you pray a prayer like that? It's totally OK to go away and think and come back to this... don't get into saying things to God just because you feel you should.

Here's space to say what you think and feel and do next:

BACKTRACK BOX ◄───────────────────

Take a ten minute walk round your block. Look, listen ~ and pray as you go…

> Be smart about this! Go in daylight and stick to where there are lots of people… or go with someone else… or if that still doesn't feel safe, go on a virtual walk – close your eyes and imagine yourself strolling the streets!

are there other houses…?

Ask God to bless the people who live in your block, even if you don't know who they are!

are there shops, pubs, offices…?

Pray about what goes on there ~

are there places for people, like schools, hospitals, day centres, churches…?

Pray that people will get helped and healed ~

are there problems…?

Ask God to get involved!

— BACKTRACK BOX ◄──

Next stop on this track: 57

From the second the alarm goes off, you're making choices ~ from 'How long can I lie here before someone drags me out of bed?' and 'Which bit of underwear shall I put on?' to big stuff, like decisions @ school which will affect your future ~ or how to act in a tricky situation with your friends…

So what are you like with those bigger choices? Put a cross somewhere along each line to show what's true for you ~

I take ages making a decision.

| Yep, that's me… | No way! |

I go with what I feel is right.

| Yep, that's me… | No way! |

I like to get all the facts first.

| Yep, that's me… | No way! |

I choose the risky options.

| Yep, that's me… | No way! |

I ask other people's advice.

| Yep, that's me… | No way! |

I ask God's advice.

| Yep, that's me… | No way! |

How you make choices is partly down to the kind of person you are. And the kind of choice you're making:

- **sometimes** choices are about finding out ~ and acting on ~ what God has to say ~ whether or not to nick stuff from a shop isn't a tough choice when you know the Bible says it's not on!

- **sometimes** God will show you very clearly what to do ~ usually with the really big stuff in your life. Maybe that's already happened for you…?

- **sometimes** God lets us make a choice ~ if he wanted to tell us what to do the whole time, he'd have made us robots!

But God *always, always* wants us to talk our choices through with him. Let's do it!

What choices have you got coming up? Put each situation in a separate box (leave out the one about your choice of underwear, though!). Then talk with God about those decisions ~ maybe pray the words in the middle, too.

LORD,

tell me your ways.

Show me how to live.

Guide me in your truth,

and teach me,

my God,

my Saviour.

[David ~ Psalm 25:4–5]

BACKTRACK BOX

Now turn back over the page ~ you've been asking God's advice and, if you want to make it a habit, put a new cross along that line...

Backtrack again over your last six prayer stops, looking for:
• what God has said;
• what God has done;
• what God wants you to *keep* praying about…
… and fill in the boxes as you go.

Now think a bit ~ God has been answering your prayers, right? And talking to you? And helping you? So what does all that tell you about him?

Turn what you've learnt about God into a praise-prayer:

Father God, I love it about you that you are…

Now say it, sing it, dance it, play it, draw it with everything you've got… he deserves it!

"All the Christians I know are total geeks! I don't want to end up with one of *them*…"

"Is it OK to go out with someone who isn't yet a Christian?"

"I just don't feel ready to go out with anyone."

"Nobody ever seems to be interested in me."

"All my mates have girl/boyfriends. I feel really lonely."

"When somebody finishes with you, it hurts like mad."

"I'm scared they'll say NO."

"I get pressured into things I don't really want to do."

"Sometimes I wonder if I'm gay."

"I feel ugly. Who's going to look at *me*?"

What goes round *your* head about the whole boyfriend/girlfriend thing…? Whatever it is, I guess you keep it pretty much to yourself… and I wonder if you think God isn't interested? Well, he is. Very.

Write God a letter, saying what gets to you about relationships ~ you'll get so much more understanding and help from God than fron *any* magazine problem page!

Dear Father God,

Love from

Talk this through with someone you can trust, too ~ choose someone with more life experience than you. God might well speak to you *through* another person.

BACKTRACK BOX

You are treasure.
You are such precious treasure.
What you bring
to the world
is beyond price.
You are totally unique treasure.
There is not
There has never been
There will never be
Anyone quite like you.

You are treasure.

That's the total truth. So let's hunt your treasure!

Ask God to show you what's special about you. Go out and live 24 hours…
then come back and say what you find.

clue
What do you do that's positive? It doesn't have to be anything heroic ~ a smile
makes a difference!

clue
What do you do well?

clue
Whose lives are better because they know you?

What do you want to say to God about this?

PS Is there anything you keep meaning to be or do, but you just don't seem to get round to it?! (Me too!) That's like burying our treasure ~ so let's get it out and let it shine!

BACKTRACK BOX ◄────────────────

Next stop on this track: 61

Are you ready for a stunningly powerful prayer for your friends? There's something special about praying the prayers in the Bible ~ and this is a *huge* one. We've changed it a bit from the Bible text so that you can say it for your mates.

So, just choose two friends and write their names in the gaps. Then pray this prayer out loud for each of your mates ~

I ask you, Father, in your great glory to give
_____ and _____ the power to be
strong inwardly through your Spirit.

   I pray that Christ will live in _____ and
_____'s hearts by faith and that their lives
will be strong in love and be built on love.

   And I pray that _____ and _____
and all God's holy people will have the power to
understand the greatness of Christ's love – how
wide and how long and how high and how deep that
love is. Christ's love is greater than anyone can ever
know, but I pray that _____ and _____
will be able to know that love. Then _____ and
_____ can be filled with your fullness, Lord.

   With your power working in us, Lord, you can
do much, much more than anything we can ask or
imagine.

   To you be the glory in the church and in
Christ Jesus for all time, for ever and ever. Amen.

[Paul, writing to some Christians in Ephesus ~ Ephesians 3:16–21]

Bring it on, Lord!!!

[me, writing to you…!]

WOW!!! Did you get that…?

If you really get into this, keep praying it for other people you're close to ~ it'd be great to pray it for yourself, too!

There are *loads* more great prayers in the Bible. Here are just a few. Check some of them out, write them here ~ and pray them for people you care about.

Philippians 1:9–11   Romans 15:13   1 Thessalonians 3:11–13   Colossians 1:3, 9–12

BACKTRACK BOX

Who in your family *seriously* gets on your nerves? If being annoying was an Olympic event, who would be up there with a medal?!

Think of two or three of your relatives you don't get on so well with, or who make you feel scared that you share some of the same DNA! Put their names or sketch them or stick their pictures in these boxes ~

I bet you're right. I bet they *are* dead irritating. But I bet there's good stuff about them, too… you might need to *really* think about this, but say what's good about those guys in these boxes. Come on, you can do it!

IMPORTANT PS

We're talking the borrowing-your-stuff-without-asking, embarrassing-you-in-front-of-your-friends level of annoying here. If something goes on with someone else in your family which is bullying or abuse or neglect, *get help* from someone you trust ~ *fast*.

So let's get talking with God about this:

step one: the good stuff
It's easy to just see the *negative* side of these people… so spend time thanking God for what's good about each of them ~

step two: the bad stuff
Tell God about what really gets to you about these people ~

step three: the tricky stuff
The truth is, we can't control those people ~ God may well get to work on them, but he might get to work on you, too. Because be honest ~ you're not all that lovely when you're wound up, are you?!

So own up to God about what you do or say when you're annoyed which isn't that great ~ tell him you're sorry. And ask for his help to be different.

BACKTRACK BOX

Sad fact: bullies get at most people some time in their lives. They might hit you, push you, trip you or pinch you. They might call you names, start rumours or threaten you. They might take your stuff, your money or your friends.

If you've ever been treated like that, write about it here ~ say what happened and how you felt.

toolkit

Being bullied is *horrible*. Here are tools to use if it happens to you ~ or to one of your friends. This isn't a choose-the-ones-you-like-best toolkit ~ you'll need them all!

· get help
  · it *won't* just go away. Tell an adult ~ like your mum or dad, youth leader or form tutor. Tell them face-to-face, by e-mail or send them a note.

· be smart
  · know where the bullies hang out ~ and don't go there alone;
  · don't hit back ~ it'll get *you* into trouble and make the bullies treat you worse;
  · try not to show your feelings ~ they'll get bored if they're not getting to you.

· remember who you are:
- bullies can make you feel really bad about yourself ~ but the truth is that the Maker of the whole universe thinks you're *fantastic*! And his opinion has to be worth more than *theirs*…!

· and pray:
- ask for God's help
  and
- this is a toughie ~ pray for the bullies. Firstly because anybody who gets a kick out of making other people feel bad *needs* help, right? But mostly because Jesus said, 'Pray for those who hurt you' [Matthew 5:44] ~ and when he asks us to do something, it's important.

Here's your space to say what you talk over with God next.

```
┌─ BACKTRACK BOX ◄──────────────────────────────┐
│                                                │
│                                                │
│                                                │
│                                                │
│                                                │
└────────────────────────────────────────────────┘
```

Next stop on this track: 64

Are you a get-up-and-get-at-it person? Or more of the long-snooze-and-lie-in type? Whatever, God wants us to have rest ~ and not just a good night's sleep or sitting-doing-nothing time…

It's like this: with God we can really rest because we have:

- no need to worry   Jesus has even beaten death!
                           [2 Timothy 1:9–10]

- nothing to prove   Jesus has made us totally OK with God
                           [Colossians 2:13–14]

- a future which is safe   Jesus gives us life forever
                           [John 3:16]

And actually, when you think about it, that's awesome. There are loads of people:

• trying hard to be good enough for God.

• feeling they'll *never* be good enough for God.

• hoping they'll be good enough for heaven.

And we really don't have to. Because through living as a human, dying on a cross and coming to life again **Jesus** has done it all for us ~ how amazingly, mind-blowingly loving is that?!

So take some time to look again at each of those three facts about rest. Thank God for those you feel confident about. Then ask him to *really* help you get to grips with the rest (and the *rest*!!)

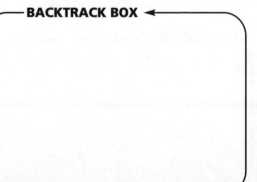

BACKTRACK BOX

Do the backtrack thing again! Go back over your last six prayer stops and fill in the **Backtrack boxes**, talking with God as you go.

So how's praying for you at the moment? Are you buzzing about all that God is doing? Or struggling to keep going? You'll experience both in your prayer-friendship with God. Struggling-to-keep-going times are *not* wrong, but they are tough. Real-life stories about God doing things through prayer can really help you get through them.

So think of four going-for-it Christians you know. Get them to text you, tell you or mail you their answers to prayer. Here's your space to write them in ~

Do this even if you're doing great at the moment ~ you'll need the encouragement some time!

Backtrack again after 6 more prayer stops @ 63

Turn on the TV. Switch on the news ~ what's happening in your country today? Write or draw the headlines in this space:

You might be too young to vote, but here's how you join with millions of other Christians to change history…!

pray about each of the situations in the headlines ~
think about what's needed… and be specific in what you say to God…

and

pray for rulers and for all who have authority ~
like politicians, the government…

> so that we can have quiet and peaceful lives
> full of worship and respect for God.
> [Paul's first letter to Timothy ~ 1 Timothy 2:2]

— BACKTRACK BOX ◄—

Next stop on this track: 67

the bad news is...

...that when you're going for it with God, his enemy (the devil) *will* try and get at you. Sorry, but that's just how it is. [Jesus told us that himself ~ check it out in Matthew 5:11 and John 15:20.]

Here's what might happen:

- you feel tempted to do things
  you *know* aren't great ~

- people give you a hard time for
  being a Christian ~

- people pressure you *not* to get
  so involved in church and stuff ~

- you have negative thoughts, like
  'all this praying is getting me
  nowhere...'

So be smart and think ~ are things like
that happening to *you*...? Use the space
to say *exactly* what is going on in your life.

But it's not *all* bad because...

...the fantastically good news is...

...that God has given us weapons to fight back, like:

It'll really help to write these verses out!

- truth – you'll have some lies thrown at you, so it's great to know what's right. [Hebrews 4:12] ~

- words to say [Luke 21:15] ~

- a way out when we're tempted [1 Corinthians 10:13] ~

AND

- prayer ~ there's a line in a song which goes, 'every prayer's a powerful weapon.' That's totally the truth!! So come on! Let's *pray*!!! Stand up and walk about as you pray for *all* you need to do what's *right* where God's enemy is trying to take you out!

Here's space to say what you do and say to God next ~

PS

It might be a battle, but guess who's *already* won?!

BACKTRACK BOX

US2

I think a lot of the time when people bully you it's God's enemy using them to try and get you to react – to try and get you to swear or do something that God doesn't want you to do. So sometimes you just need to recognise what it is and pray against that. *Jamie*

Next stop on this track: 68

Anybody ever accuse you of having 'an attitude'? The truth is that you've got *lots* of attitudes! Here are just some of them ~

Me first.	I want the best for other people.
I want to help.	I feel like covering up the wrong things I do.
I feel jealous.	I think I'm better than….
I want to get my own back.	I want to do the right thing.
I feel *mad*…	I want more and more and more and…
I feel like causing trouble.	I want to please God.

- **sort** ~ whizz through that list and underline the **God**-attitudes in one colour… and the **me**-attitudes in another.

- **know yourself** ~ circle two **God**-attitudes *you* have… then circle two **me**-attitudes *you* get sometimes.

- **understand** ~ **actions** come from **attitudes**, so if you sort the **attitude**, the **action** usually follows! [To get this idea, just choose one attitude ~ think what you might do if you felt that way…]

- **pray** ~

Me-*attitudes*
- Own up to God about the ones you've circled.
- Tell God you're sorry…
- If you want to change, choose *now* to put those attitudes out of your life ~ and ask God to help.

God-*attitudes*
- Thank God for the ones you've circled.
- Choose now to work on these attitudes ~ and ask God to grow them in you.
- Choose another God-attitude which you don't think you have yet, and ask for God's help to grow that, too.

Or look at it this way...

You're probably not much into gardening! OK, but you know plants have roots, right? The roots are like our attitudes ~ you *can't* see them, but you *can* see what grows out of them! And, if you want to get rid of something you don't like, you need to dig right down to the roots...

> Be careful what you think, because your thoughts run your life
> [Proverbs 4:23]

Get a plant for your room. Every time you look at it, pray again about *your* 'roots' ~ the attitudes which make you do what you do.

Us2

I prayed for willpower, like for when you come to revise and you don't really want to? You look around and there's a million and one other things you could do ~ you could see if there's anything good on TV, listen to some music, go on the computer – anything! I just prayed that God would give me the willpower to say, 'OK I'm going to sit down and I'm going to do this'. And that's working quite well for me at the moment.   *Hayley*

I used to be bullied, but that wasn't the main issue for me ~ someone would say something and I'd just turn around and hit them. That was partly the way I'd been brought up, so I'd get into fights all the time. God has taken all that away.   *Jamie*

BACKTRACK BOX ◄

Next stop on this track: 69

Sx msgs ~ there are loads of them about. You get them from books, magazines, music, films, TV... You get them at school, at home, at church... So *who* says *what* about *when* it's OK to have sex? Scribble down *all* the ideas you've heard ~ even if you don't agree with them!

it's OK to have sex when...   **says who..?**

A bit confusing, isn't it...?!

Well, what God says is totally clear ~ sex is a *beautiful* thing, designed for two people who are totally sold out for each other in a marriage relationship. Anything else is *so* much less than the best for us.

It's as simple as that.

The whole sex thing might seem as far off as the next solar system at the moment...! But make your choices *now* and pray them into your life. You *could* do this with your best friend ~ and someone with a bit more life experience than you.

Go with what God says or go with what everybody else says....?

Get this: what goes on in your own secret world is important, too. There's loads of stuff on TV, in magazines, movies and music which will get you thinking about sex ~ what are you going to do about that...?

If you're in a relationship, hold onto these three simple guidelines: don't get horizontal + don't touch the bits you haven't got + if your feelings start running away with you ~ STOP.

Remember: if you've done things you now regret, tell God about it ~ you'll get total forgiveness and a completely fresh start! [1 John 1:9] Don't keep making the same mistakes, though...

Here's your space to put down what you think:

Now tell God what *you've* decided. Ask – and keep asking! – for his help to stick to it ~ you're really going to need it…!

BACKTRACK BOX ◄

You've seen those movies where the main character looks like a normal kid at school, but really he's somebody else ~ like Spiderman? Well, that's you. Yes, *you!* You might *look like* most other teenagers, but you're really something else... You are:

- a child of God ~ so you're loved by God himself!
    [John 1:12–13]
- a royal priest ~ so you're God's chosen representative!
    [1 Peter 2:9]
- an heir with Jesus ~ so Jesus shares *everything* he has with you!
    [Romans 8:17]
- a temple of the Holy Spirit ~ so the total power of God is living in you!
    [1 Corinthians 6:19]

Wow. I mean, seriously ~ **WOW**.

That's mind-blowing, isn't it?! So, take time to think about each of those things in God's company. Remember, you haven't *earned* any of them ~ they're all God's *gifts* to you in Jesus.

What do you want to say to God about all of this?

big, important prayer
Ask God to help you live this out, 24–7 ~

Design a symbol for each of those four things you *are* (priest, heir etc). For a symbol, you need to draw something very simple...

child of God: *royal priest:*

heir with Jesus: *temple of the Holy Spirit:*

Then try out different ways of working the symbols into your name. Maybe link them all together and draw them by the side or underneath your name. Or maybe they can become part of some of the letters...?

From now on, whenever you write or sign your name, add the symbols – to remind you of who you *really* are.

BACKTRACK BOX

Picture this: it's your birthday and you're ready to party! Who would you invite? Write a guest list here.

And who would *never* get an invitation? Be honest…write the names of a few people you would *not* invite *here*.

Of course, you can't have *everybody* at a party… but let's think about these un-friends for a minute ~ what is it about them that you don't like?

The thing is, Jesus asks us to *love* people ~ even those we don't particularly *like!* Obviously that *totally* rules out:

- prejudice because of someone's background

- treating the Billy and Bella No-Friends of this world like everybody else does…

So are you ready for a challenge?

step one: pray
Talk with God honestly about your un-friends. (Are there any wrong attitudes you need him to sort?)

step two: walk the talk
In other words, *do* something! Think of what you could say or do to make contact with your un-friends. Start small. Here's your space to say what you decide ~ and what happens…

But before you do *anything* – *pray*!

---BACKTRACK BOX ◄─────────────────────────

Backtrack... think... write... pray!

Talking and sharing stuff with your friends brings you closer, right? Talking and sharing stuff with God in prayer brings you closer to him, too.

Try and remember what your relationship with God was like when you started this journal ~ and think about how it's changed...

Here's your space to say how it is with you and God *now*:
• Use pictures and images
• Or use words to write a poem or a song or a letter
• Or describe it as a dance or a mime.

Did you know:

- the average person will spend two weeks of their life kissing?
- cockroaches can survive for extended periods of time without their heads?
- a sneeze can travel at 100 mph?
- crocodiles can't stick their tongues out?
- if you yelled for 8 years, 7 months and 3 days you'd produce enough sound energy to heat a cup of coffee?

You're learning things all the time – in and out of school. But not every bit of info which comes our way is useful! Let's focus on the *really* important stuff ~

What have *you* learnt about God recently?

> **PRAY!**
> Thank God for what he has taught you...!

God has loads of *vital* stuff to teach us. And you'll find masses of it in the Bible. We're not talking about cramming our heads with a bunch of who-did-what-and-where Bible facts... we're talking about learning stuff that can *transform* us ~

Can you spot...

1 source for everything the Scriptures say ~ that's the Bible to you and me!

7 things the Bible can do for you?

4 ways to get the most out of it?

> You should continue following the teachings you learnt. You know they are true, because you trust those who taught you. Since you were a child you have known the Holy Scriptures which are able to make you wise. And that wisdom leads to salvation through faith in Christ Jesus. All Scripture is given by God and is useful for teaching, for showing people what is wrong in their lives, for correcting faults and for teaching how to live right. Using the Scriptures, the person who serves God will be capable, having all that is needed to do every good work.
>
> [Paul's second letter to Timothy ~ 2 Timothy 3:14–17]

> **PRAY!**
> Ask God to help you see the Bible like this... and use it to the max.

So here's some Bible text ~ read it like it's a really important message from God to you ~

> Trust the Lord with all your heart,
> and don't depend on your own understanding.
> Remember the Lord in all you do,
> and he will give you success.
> Don't depend on your own wisdom.
> Respect the Lord and refuse to do wrong.
>
> [Proverbs 3:5–7]

PRAY!
Ask God to speak through this Bible text... what is he saying to you?

PRAY!
Talk honestly with God about cutting out time to get into the Bible.

Let's not leave learning about God in the Bible somewhere on our to-do list ~ it's way too important for that! You'll need to make quality space for it. So...

Hey ~ why not write bits of Bible text which are really special to you inside the covers of this journal!

BACKTRACK BOX ◄

Jesus said, 'I came to give life – life in all its fullness.' [John 10:10]

Did you get that? Jesus *is* talking about the life you'll enjoy for ever with God in heaven… but he also means *your* life *right here*, *right now*. Sure, it's hard sometimes. And there are *huge* challenges. But being a Christian should mean living life to the *max*!

Or look at it like this: life with God is a bit like a roller-coaster ride ~ there are ups and there are downs ~ but the *whole* thing is fantastic!

So think a bit ~ does being a Christian *feel* like 'life in all its fullness'…?

☑   Excellent! Thank God for the life he's given you!

☒   Talk with God honestly about what's wrong ~ he'll really want to sort whatever it is…

Write whatever you say to God about your life with him along this roller-coaster line ~

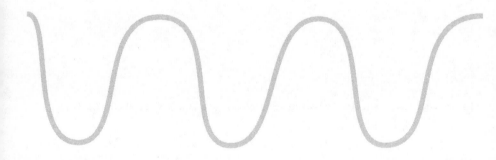

BACKTRACK BOX ◄

In the prayer Jesus taught us, there's a line which goes:

> Give us today our daily bread..

You'll *probably* get bread today… and crisps… and chocolate… and chips… and a whole lot of other delish stuff! Take a minute to write or draw everything you've eaten – or will eat – today on this plate: *****

Thank God for today's food

Now think of a person or a group of people who *won't* get the food they need today ~ write their name(s) or paste their picture on this plate.

Get those people in your mind ~ and pray *hard*. Use Jesus' words to start with…

> Our Father in heaven ~
> Give us the food we need for each day
> [Matthew 6:11]

Maybe this prayer will get you doing something…?

*If food is an issue for you, get help from someone you trust ~ *fast*.

— BACKTRACK BOX ◄

6 296 213 109

That's how many people there are in the world today. And you're just one of them! As you look around at what the other 6 296 213 108 people are up to, what makes you happy? And what doesn't?

I'm glad about...   I'm sad about...

OK, so you're only 1 in over 6,000 million... and those are probably *mega* issues.

But **God** *is* **Lord of the whole Universe**... and **he answers prayer**, right?!

So *pray* ~

Thank God for the good things ~ (maybe the end to a war or a medical breakthrough...)

Use your mind to pray about the sad things ~ think about what's *needed* in a situation (like aid to get to starving people...) and ask God for it.

Is it true today
that when people pray
cloudless skies will break
kings and queens will shake?
yes it's true and I believe it
I'm living for you

I'm gonna be a history maker in this land
I'm gonna be a speaker of truth to all
mankind...

Written by Martin Smith,
© Curious? Music. Rights administered by Bucks Music Ltd.
Lyrics reproduced by permission.

How about you?

And you could also:

- choose an issue you feel really strongly about... get a pin board for your room and make it a prayer-site... surf the net for information and cut out magazine or newspaper headlines and pin them up... add notes of what you pray and what happens... update it with new info every week...

- find a charity which is out there, hands on, doing something about it... get yourself involved... if it's a Christian charity, they'll have a prayer letter to help you pray...!

- watch a news bulletin... pray the whole way through... pray for every situation as it comes up...

- check out www.24–7Prayer.com... it's a site for young people who want to pray and make a difference... is that you?

- get some friends together to pray about what's going on in the world... have lots of info ready... start with 30 minutes... next time, try an hour...

— BACKTRACK BOX ◄—

You: I'm, er, I'm a Christian…

Someone else: You're a *what?!*

You: I'm a Christian.

Someone else: What do you want
to be one of those for?!

You: Er…

> Always be ready to answer
> everyone who asks you to
> explain about the hope you
> have, but answer in a gentle
> way and with respect…
>
> [1 Peter 3:15–16]

If you're going for it with God, people around you are going to notice. And one day, someone will ask you what the deal is. Are you ready? Do you know what to say?

They're not looking for a sermon. They're not looking for you to prove God exists. All you need to do is say why you're following Jesus ~ and what difference it makes to your life. Simple, eh? So let's give it a go:

• Say why you became a Christian ~

• Say how you became a Christian ~

• Say what's good about being a
  Christian ~

• Use simple words that everyone will understand. I've heard people say they've been 'washed in the blood of the Lamb' ~ yes… but tell that to your mates, they'll think you've totally lost it!

- *Have enough words ready to last about a minute ~ they don't need your whole life story!*

- *Learn it ~ not like a speech, but so that you can be relaxed saying it when you get the chance!*

Ready? Fantastic! Now *pray*:
- Ask God to give you a chance to tell someone your story.
- Ask for his help to overcome your nerves (they're normal!).

Here's space for what you say to God.

BACKTRACK BOX

Jesus said, "All power in heaven and on earth is given to me. So go and make followers of all people in the world…"

[Matthew 28:18–19]

Starring in a movie... playing in a band... winning an Olympic gold... when you're sitting at school in your *dullest* lesson, what do *you* dream about?

And what are your *hopes* for the future? Think this year... but also try and think into your twenties! Think what you'd like to do... where you'd like to be... who you'd like to be with...

God once told a bunch of people, 'I have *good* plans for you' ~ and that's true for us, too. That doesn't mean God has planned out your life in what-you're-going-to-eat-for-breakfast detail. But it does mean he has some special stuff in store for you...

See Jeremiah 29:11, if you want to check it out!

So talk with God about this ~

Take time to tell him about your hopes and dreams…

… and here's what you *could* do next ~ but think first. Hold out this book like you're giving God those hopes and dreams. Some of them will be things God wants for you, too… but he *might* take some of them away ~ are you ready for that?

This is a *big* and *really powerful* prayer ~ it's you saying, 'I'm giving you my life, Lord. I'm trusting you know what's best for me…' If you mean it, here's your space to say it in your own words ~

BACKTRACK BOX

'God will either give you what you ask – or something far better.'

[Robert Murray M'Cheyne]

backtrack one
Re-trace your steps over those last six prayer stops. Listen to God and talk with him as you go. And use the boxes to say what's going on in the situations you've prayed about.

backtrack two
Make yourself comfy… get yourself something to drink… turn off your mobile… shut the door…

Go right back to the beginning of this journal. Look at what you've prayed… look at what God's done… look at how you've changed…

Fantastic, eh? When you get back here, use this space to say or draw what you're thinking and feeling…

Is that it, then?
Are we done with praying? *No way!!!*
This is just the beginning! So make a plan to keep it going…
… like how about getting yourself a really nice notebook? Have a double page for each prayer stop you make ~ use the left-hand side for what you pray… and the right-hand side for how God answers. You could use the tracks we've followed ~ if you like being organised, go through and write a title on each page! Oh, and remember to backtrack often ~ or you might miss what God is doing!

> Pray continually, and give thanks, whatever happens. This is what God wants for you in Christ Jesus.
> [1 Thessalonians 5:17]

Here's space for *anything* you want to say to God ~ like when something great happens, or when your day is pants and you just want to let off steam! There's room for Bible texts, ideas, messages, songs, pictures… it's your space!

Us2

It was my mum's wedding a few months ago. She's strongly anti-Christian and it's always tough for me because she always ridicules me. But before I went I just prayed, 'I know this is going to be a really tough couple of days, can you just help me through somehow?' I ended up sitting next to this man for the entire reception who was a Christian. That was just really amazing because he must be the only Christian my mum knows! *Jamie*

Text for a tough day

He says, "Don't be afraid,
because I have saved you.
I have called you by name,
and you are mine.
When you pass through the
waters, I will be with you.
When you cross rivers, you
will not drown.
When you walk through fire
you will not be burnt,
nor will the flames hurt you.
This is because I, the Lord,
am your God,
the Holy One of Israel, your
Saviour."

[Isaiah 43:1–3]

Text for a great day

My whole being, praise
the Lord;
all my being, praise his
holy name.
My whole being, praise
the Lord
and do not forget all
his kindnesses.

[Psalm 103:1,2]

help! What do I pray if someone gets really ill...?

Simple: pray your heart out for the person to get better. God *does* heal. Sometimes it happens here and now ~ maybe miraculously, maybe through medicine. But understand that *sometimes* his healing *only* comes in the new body we have when, as Christians, we go to be with him ~ check out Revelation 21:3–5 and I Corinthians 15:42–44.

The questions and feelings you get when something bad is happening to someone you love are tough ~ really tough. Don't go through them alone. Talk ~ and keep talking! ~ to friends, family, people @ church or teachers you trust. It's really hard if healing isn't happening in the way you've asked, but keep praying, too ~ God wants to hear and to help when you feel sad, disappointed, confused or even mad at him ~ if you're not sure about that, just have a quick flick through the Psalms!

US2

I didn't mean to, but I hurt someone badly ~ he went deaf in one ear. And I prayed. The next day he was absolutely fine. And he even forgave me, which was a big deal... *Rachel*